GRAPHIC ORGANIZERS AND PLANNING OUTLINES

for Authentic Instruction and Assessment

by Imogene Forte
and Sandra Schurr

Incentive Publications, Inc.
Nashville, Tennessee

Cover by Marta Drayton and Joe Shibley
Edited by Jan Keeling

ISBN 0-86530-347-9

PRINTED IN THE UNITED STATES OF AMERICA

Table of Contents

PREFACE

It's time to organize and to learn! In this book you will find useful forms, planning outlines, and graphic organizers. These are all learning aids whose effectiveness depends on visual organization of information. For most people, graphic organizers are easier to grasp—and remember—than are extended blocks of text. There are three basic ways to use a graphic organizer in the classroom.

- When it's time to plan a lesson, study for a test, write a paper, plan a performance, or create a project, student or teacher may *begin* with a graphic organizer and use it to stay on track.

- A graphic organizer can be created *as learning progresses,* in which case it becomes an aid to learning.

- A third approach is to create a graphic organizer *after* knowledge is acquired, using it to present newly learned information.

Eight major sections present eight different types of reproducible outlines and organizers, with instructions to be found on the first few pages of each section. With the exception of two content-specific forms (page 27 and page 60), the outlines and organizers may be used in all content areas. A few of the organizers, for which patterns cannot be easily standardized, are presented as pages with instructions and illustrations. These may also be reproduced if desired. All instructions are written in the second person and indicate whether the organizer is intended for teacher or student use, or for both. It should be noted that many of the student pages work just as well for teachers!

The eight sections include:

Charts, Graphs, and Grids

A chart may be essential in keeping track of related ideas, hanging on to thoughts that need to be remembered, or scheduling and tracking time and activities.

Cognitive Taxonomy Outlines

This section presents easy outlines for comprehension and use of three important cognitive taxonomies: Howard Gardner's Multiple Intelligences, Williams' Taxonomy of Divergent Thinking and Feeling, and Bloom's Taxonomy of Cognitive Development. Accompanying the information are lesson-planning forms for each taxonomy.

Forms for Group Learning

These outlines and organizers are designed to be used in cooperative learning groups.

Forms for Interdisciplinary Teaching

Interdisciplinary teaching becomes easier to manage with the aid of these forms and organizers.

Planning Forms and Outlines

These planning sheets will enhance learning. Three forms to make parent/student/teacher conferences go more smoothly are included.

Research and Study Aids

Graphic organizers and forms can make the research process less intimidating and can be invaluable aids to study as well.

The Web

A web is a graphic organizer that begins with a central idea placed in a prominent place, with supporting ideas arranged around the central idea, generally connected to the center with lines. Such a structure provides the student with a graphic portrayal of ideas and their relationships to one another. A classic web is shown on page 79, while variations appear on pages 80 through 84.

Writing Planners and Organizers

Student work will improve when these organizers are used to aid the writing of book reports, novels, reports, and other assignments.

The forms and organizers are valuable assessment tools. Many of the teacher evaluation forms can be used to assess student work, while the student forms and organizers will help students arrange and present work in their assessment portfolios.

Packed with clever organizing tools, this is a book to be used by teachers and students for countless purposes in all content areas . . . over and over again!

Charts, Graphs, and Grids

Page 11

Decision Chart

For Students

The Decision Chart is helpful when you have to make a decision and you don't know quite where to begin. In the DECISION rectangle at the top of the page, write a brief statement that describes the nature of the decision you must make. Then, in the ALTERNATIVE IDEAS column, list a number of alternative ideas that could resolve your dilemma. Then decide on a set of criteria to be used in judging the worth of each alternative idea and list these in the slanted boxes labeled CRITERIA. Rate each individual criterion according to the scoring scale as shown. Finally, compile the total score for each alternative idea. The best decision is probably the idea that has the highest point value!

Page 12

Graph Matrix

For Students

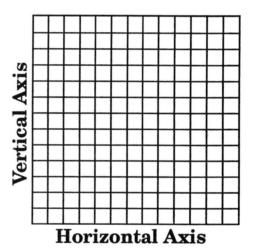

The Graph Matrix is a starter matrix to use when constructing a bar graph or a line graph on a topic of your choice. Put one set of descriptors on the vertical axis and another set of descriptors on the horizontal axis to show the relationship between the two categories. For example, if you want to make a bar graph that shows the relationship of the earth's population growth to the passage of time, you might label the vertical axis "Earth's Population in Millions" and the horizontal axis "Time (Centuries)." Be sure to write a title for your graph on the line at the top of the page.

Page 13

Multi-Puzzle Grid

For Students

This blank grid can be used for constructing crossword puzzles or wordfind puzzles. If designing a crossword puzzle, make a list of clues for words, write the words in appropriate squares on the grid, and black in the blank squares. To make a wordfind puzzle, use a separate piece of paper to list words related to a theme or topic. Fill appropriate squares with letters that form these words, then add other letters at random to the blank squares.

9

Decision Chart

Directions on page 9

Decision to be made

Criteria

Total Scores

Alternative Ideas

1.
2.
3.
4.
5.
6.
7.
8.
9.
10.

Scoring of criteria: 3 points = Great
2 points = O.K.
1 point   = Not so good

Directions on page 9

Graph Matrix

Title: _____

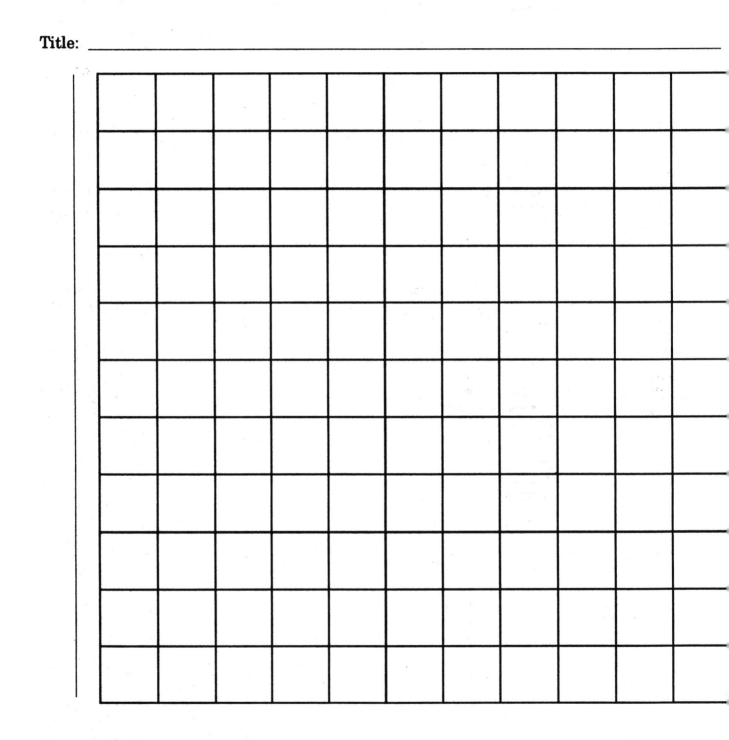

Directions on page 9

Multi-Puzzle Grid

Title: _____

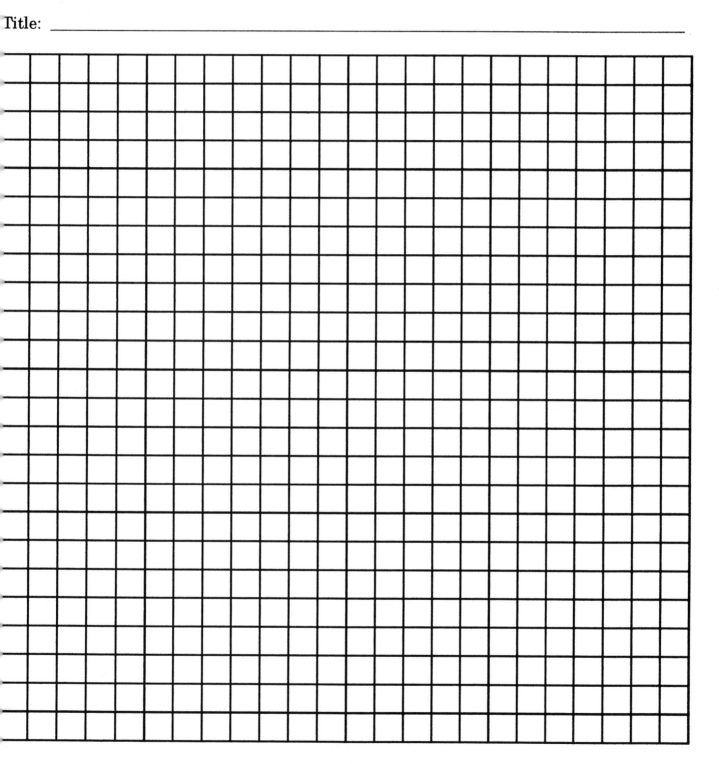

Directions on page 10

Problem-Solution Boxes

PROBLEM   HOW SOLVED

Thought-a-Day Calendar

Directions on page 10

Sunday	Monday	Tuesday	Wednesday	Thursday	Friday	Saturday

Directions on page 10

Reading Record

Name _____

Date		Title of Book	Pages Read	New and Different Words
1.				
2.				
3.				
4.				
5.				
6.				
7.				
8.				
9.				

Directions on page 10

Classroom Chart

Directions on page 10

Substitute Teacher's Daily Schedule

Time	Activity	Materials, Textbooks, and Page Numbers

Have a great day!
Please leave notes about the day here:

Cognitive Taxonomy Outlines

Page 21

An Introduction to the Multiple Intelligences

For Students

This page will introduce students to Dr. Howard Gardner's Theory of Multiple Intelligences. Each student should be given a copy of the page, since lines are provided for student self-assessment.

Page 22

Multiple Intelligences Lesson Plan

For Teachers

Use this chart when planning a lesson or a unit whose activities should be balanced among the seven intelligences. To make sure that every student in the class is given the chance to use his or her strengths, refer to the student self-assessment sheets based on page 21.

Page 23

Williams' Taxonomy

For Teachers

The Williams model can be used to develop creative activity when planning tasks and assignments. The levels of this taxonomy are defined as skills and include cue words that will help trigger the desired behavior.

Page 24

Williams' Taxonomy Lesson Plan

For Teachers

Use this chart when planning a lesson or a unit whose activities should be balanced among the skills described by Williams' Taxonomy. Refer to the information on page 22 for help in developing suitable activities.

19

Page 25

Bloom's Taxonomy

For Teachers

Bloom's Taxonomy provides a way to organize thinking skills into six levels, from the first, most basic, level to the final, more complex, level of thinking.

Page 26

Do-It-Yourself Outline for Developing a Unit on Any Content Topic

For Teachers

Developing a unit on a topic of your choice is easier than you think. Just choose your topic and then select one or more tasks from each level of Bloom's Taxonomy on page 25 to create a teaching and learning unit.

Pages 27–28

Bloom's Experiment Form for Use with Any Science Topic

For Students

This two-page form based on Bloom's Taxonomy will enable you to conduct a science experiment that is methodical and comprehensive.

Graphic Organizers and Planning Outlines

Directions on page 19

An Introduction to the Multiple Intelligences

Did you know there are seven different types of intelligence? Each of us possesses all seven, although for each person one or more of them may be stronger than the others. Dr. Howard Gardner, a researcher and professor at the Harvard Graduate School of Education, developed the Theory of Multiple Intelligences to help us better understand ourselves and the way we acquire information in school.

Assign a number to each of the seven intelligences on this page to help evaluate how you learn. Your strongest intelligence area should be assigned 1 and your weakest intelligence area should be assigned 7. All others should be ranked with numbers from 2 to 6. Try to think of examples and instances in the classroom when you were successful on a test, assignment, activity, or task because it was compatible with the way you like to learn.

____ 1. **Verbal-Linguistic Intelligence**
   Do you find it easy to memorize information, write poems or stories, give talks, read books, play word games, use big words, and remember what you hear?

____ 2. **Logical-Mathematical Intelligence**
   Do you find it easy to compute math problems in your head and on paper, to solve brainteasers, to do logic puzzles, to conduct science experiments, to figure out number and sequence patterns, and to watch shows on science and nature themes?

____ 3. **Visual-Spatial Intelligence**
   Do you find it easy to draw, paint, or doodle, work through puzzles and mazes, build with blocks, and follow maps and flowcharts? Do you prefer reading material that has lots of illustrations?

____ 4. **Body-Kinesthetic Intelligence**
   Do you find it easy to engage in sports and physical activities, move around, spend free time outdoors, work with your hands on such things as model building or sewing, participate in dance, ballet, gymnastics, plays, puppet shows, or other performances, and use finger paints, clay, and papier-mâché?

____ 5. **Musical-Rhythmical Intelligence**
   Do you find it easy to play an instrument or sing, listen to favorite music, make up your own songs or raps, recognize off-key recordings or noises, remember television jingles and lyrics, and work while listening to or humming simple melodies and tunes?

____ 6. **Interpersonal Intelligence**
   Do you find it easy to make friends, meet strangers, resolve conflicts, lead groups or clubs, engage in gossip, participate in team sports, plan social activities, and teach or counsel others?

____ 7. **Intrapersonal Intelligence**
   Do you find it easy to function independently, do your own work and thinking, spend time alone, engage in solo hobbies and activities, set goals, analyze your own strengths and weaknesses, and keep private diaries or journals?

Directions on page 19

Multiple Intelligences Lesson Plan

Theme: _____

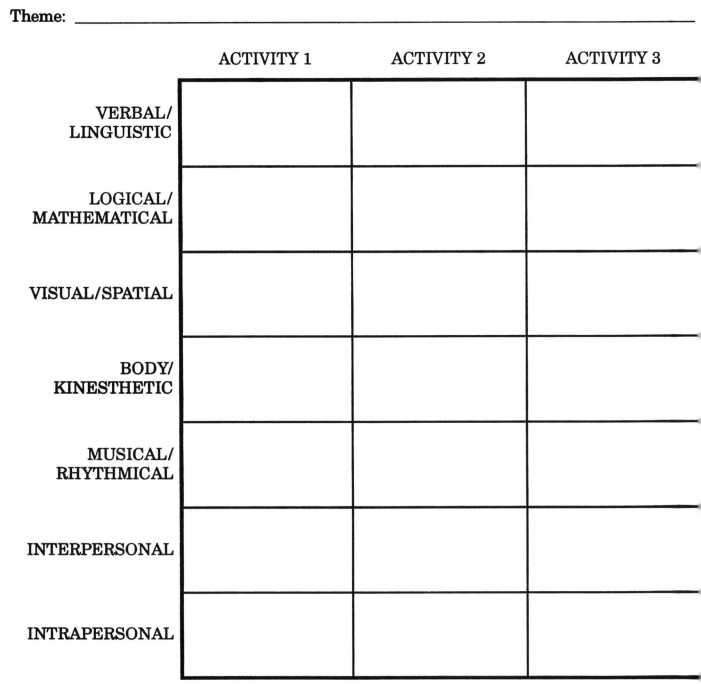

	ACTIVITY 1	ACTIVITY 2	ACTIVITY 3
VERBAL/ LINGUISTIC			
LOGICAL/ MATHEMATICAL			
VISUAL/SPATIAL			
BODY/ KINESTHETIC			
MUSICAL/ RHYTHMICAL			
INTERPERSONAL			
INTRAPERSONAL			

NOTE: Not every rectangle need be filled in for every topic. Just make sure there is a good content balance in each unit

Directions on page 19

Williams' Taxonomy

Fluency

This skill enables the learner to generate lots of ideas and a large number of choices.
   Trigger words: how many?, one, quantity, a few, oodles, a bunch, scads, lots

Flexibility

This skill enables the learner to alter everyday objects to fit a variety of categories by taking detours and varying size, shape, quantities, time limits, or dimensions in a given situation.
   Trigger words: variety, adapt, different, redirect, detour, alternatives, change

Originality

This skill enables the learner to seek the unusual by suggesting clever twists to change content or seek the novel in a given situation.
   Trigger words: unusual, unique, new, clever, not obvious, novel

Elaboration

This skill enables the learner to stretch a topic by expanding, enlarging, enriching, or embellishing a list of finds or possibilities in order to build on previous thoughts or ideas in a given situation.
   Trigger words: embellish, expand, build, embroider, stretch, enlarge, enrich, add on

Risk Taking

This skill enables the learner to deal with the unknown by taking chances, experimenting with new ideas, or trying new challenges in a given situation.
   Trigger words: dare, estimate, explore, guess, try, experiment, predict

Complexity

This skill enables the learner to create structure in an unstructured setting or to bring a logical order to a given situation.
   Trigger words: improve, seek alternatives, solve, order, intricate

Curiosity

This skill enables the learner to follow a hunch, question alternatives, ponder outcomes, and wonder about options in a given situation.
   Trigger words: question, inquire, ask, follow a hunch, wonder, puzzle, ponder

Imagination

This skill enables the learner to visualize possibilities, build images in one's mind, picture new objects, or reach beyond the limits of the practical in response to a given situation.
   Trigger words: reach, fantasize, visualize, expand, wonder, dream

Directions on page 19

Williams' Taxonomy Lesson Plan

Theme: _____

	ACTIVITY 1	ACTIVITY 2	ACTIVITY 3
FLUENCY			
FLEXIBILITY			
ORIGINALITY			
ELABORATION			
RISK TAKING			
COMPLEXITY			
CURIOSITY			
IMAGINATION			

NOTE: Not every rectangle need be filled in for every topic. Just make sure there is a good content balance in each unit.

Directions on page 20

Bloom's Taxonomy

Knowledge

At this stage the learner will be able to recall, restate, and remember learned information.

Trigger verbs: find, group, identify, label, list, memorize, outline, read, recall, what, when, where, who, write

Comprehension

At this stage the learner grasps the meaning of information by interpreting and translating what has been learned.

Trigger verbs: associate, contrast, define, estimate, explain, reorganize, retell, summarize, transform

Application

The learner makes use of information in a context different from the one in which it was learned.

Trigger verbs: apply, choose, classify, construct, employ, experiment, model, produce, prove, select, utilize

Analysis

The learner breaks learned information into its component parts.

Trigger verbs: analyze, break down, classify, compare, discover, examine, infer, simplify, sort, take apart

Synthesis

The learner creates new information and ideas using what has been previously learned.

Trigger verbs: blend, build, compose, construct, create, design, devise, imagine, invent, make up, originate

Evaluation

The learner makes judgments about learned information on the basis of established criteria.

Trigger verbs: assess, conclude, criticize, decide, defend, determine, evaluate, grade, justify, rank, recommend

Directions on page 20

Do-It-Yourself Outline for Developing a Unit on Any Content Topic

TOPIC: _____

KNOWLEDGE
1. List five to ten questions that you would like to answer about the topic.
2. Identify five to ten key words or terms related to the topic and write their definitions.
3. Name three to five specific sources for information about the topic.

COMPREHENSION
1. Outline a plan for finding out all you can about the topic.
2. Summarize what you would like to know most about the topic.
3. Describe five to ten ways that you might share acquired information.

APPLICATION
1. Interview someone with knowledge of the topic.
2. Make a model to show something important about the topic.
3. Conduct an experiment to demonstrate a key idea related to the topic.

ANALYSIS
1. Compare and contrast some aspect of your topic with that of another topic.
2. Divide your topic into several subtopics.
3. Conduct a survey to show how others feel about the topic.

SYNTHESIS
1. Create a list of predictions related to the topic.
2. Compose a poem or story about the topic.
3. Design a series of drawings or diagrams to show facts about the topic.

EVALUATION
1. Determine the five most important facts you have learned about the topic. Order them from most important to least important, giving reasons for your first choice.
2. Criticize a resource you used to find out more information about the topic and give at least three recommendations for improving it.

Directions on page 20

Bloom's Experiment Form for Use with Any Science Topic

KNOWLEDGE

List the materials used in this experiment.

Materials: _____

_____

_____

_____

COMPREHENSION

Outline the procedure for conducting this experiment.
Procedure:

1. _____
2. _____
3. _____
4. _____
5. _____
6. _____

APPLICATION

Record data observed and collected during your experiment in chart or graph form.
Data:

What I Did	What I Observed

Name _____

Directions on page 20

Bloom's Experiment Form, Page 2

ANALYSIS

Examine your data and draw conclusions.
Conclusions:

1. _____

_____

2. _____

_____

3. _____

_____

SYNTHESIS

Create a series of "what if" statements about your data to show things that might be different should variables be changed.

What if . . . _____

_____

What if . . . _____

_____

What if . . . _____

_____

EVALUATION

Describe how you would rate the success of your experiment. Establish a set of criteria for measuring the results.

What I Did	What I Observed

28

Forms for Group Learning

Page 31

Group Experiment Outline

For Students

Use this form when planning a group activity that involves observation and methodical procedures, such as a math or science experiment.

Page 32

Group Matrix Diagram

For Students

This matrix is most helpful when students want to collaborate on a project and need to develop a plan for who is going to do what. The project tasks or action steps are recorded on the left-hand side of the matrix under the TASK heading, while the names of individuals are recorded along the top of the matrix in the angled areas. Check the appropriate space(s) as each person is matched with a task or tasks.

Page 33

Group Project Plan

For Students

Use this form to clarify assignments, dates, materials needed, goals, and plan of action when beginning a group learning project.

Page 34

Group Plan at a Glance

For Teachers and Students

The information on this planning form is similar to that in the Group Project Plan on page 33, but it is presented as a graphic organizer, a more visual approach that may be desired at times.

29

Directions on page 29

Group Experiment Outline

Group: _____

Roles: _____

_____

Problem: _____

_____

Materials: _____

_____

Procedure:

Date	What We Did	What We Observed
_____	_____	_____
_____	_____	_____
_____	_____	_____
_____	_____	_____

Findings: _____

_____

_____

Conclusions: _____

_____

_____

Evaluation (including what I could have done differently and how it would have affected the experiment):

_____

_____

_____

_____

31

Directions on page 29

Group Matrix Diagram

Students

Tasks

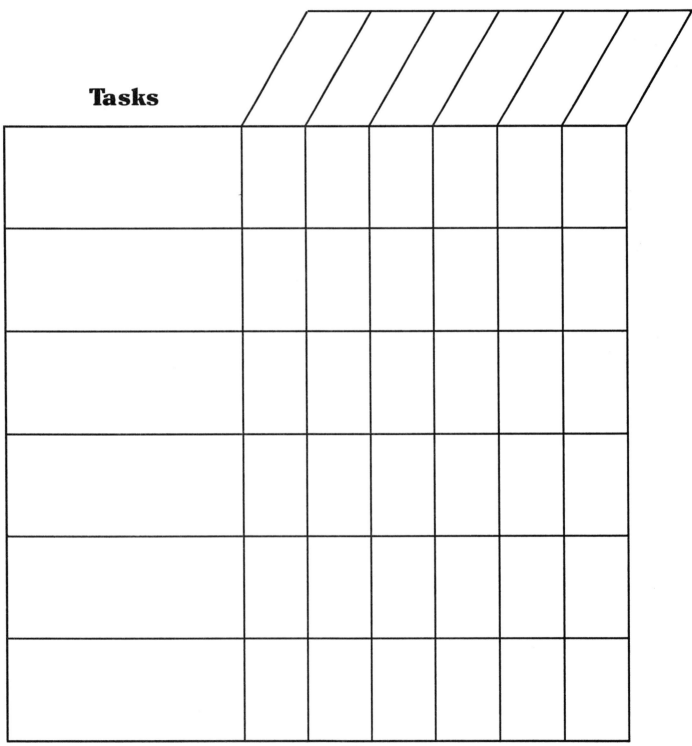

Directions on page 29

Group Project Plan

Activity:_____

Group Members: Role Assignments:

_____   _____

_____   _____

_____   _____

_____   _____

Beginning Date: _____ Completion Date: _____

Materials Needed:_____

_____

_____

Major Objective: _____

_____

_____

Learning Goals:_____

_____

_____

Plan of Action: _____

_____

_____

_____

Directions on page 29

Group Plan at a Glance
(For Teacher and Student Use)

Topic:_____ Completion Date:_____

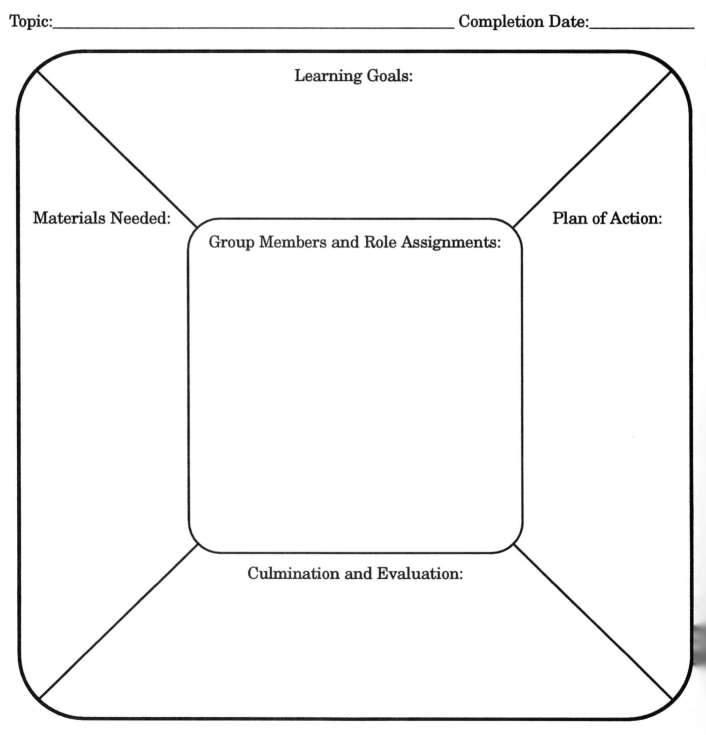

Learning Goals:

Materials Needed:

Plan of Action:

Group Members and Role Assignments:

Culmination and Evaluation:

Directions on page 30

Group Evaluation Form

Activity: _____

Group Interaction: _____

_____

Individual Contributions: _____

_____

Effectiveness of Objectives: _____

_____

Effectiveness of Action Plan: _____

_____

Applicability of Materials Selected: _____

_____

Use of Time: _____

_____

Major Problems: _____

_____

_____

Major Strengths: _____

_____

_____

Summary: _____

_____

_____

Next Time We Would: _____

_____

Signatures: _____   _____

_____   _____

_____   _____

Directions on page 30

Group Rating Scale

Activity: _____

	Excellent	Good	Fair	Poor
Group Interaction				
Individual Contributions				
Role Assignments				
Objectives				
Plan of Action				
Materials				
Use of Time				
Overall Rating				

Signatures:

_____   _____

_____   _____

_____   _____

Date: _____

Forms for Interdisciplinary Teaching

Page 39

Building an Interdisciplinary Planning Matrix

For Teachers

Members of a teaching team can use this form to list all the major concepts, units, skills, or topics each will be covering during the school year, recording by subject area and month. Look for overlapping areas that can be easily worked into interdisciplinary units.

Page 40

Interdisciplinary Tree

For Teachers

An Interdisciplinary Tree is a planning tool in the shape of a tree with a trunk and a set of roots, branches, and leaves. A teaching team uses this tree facsimile to record ideas for an interdisciplinary unit by writing the theme or topic on the trunk, the material resources on the roots, the concepts on the branches, and the related skills on the leaves. An example of a completed Interdisciplinary Tree for a unit on chocolate appears below.

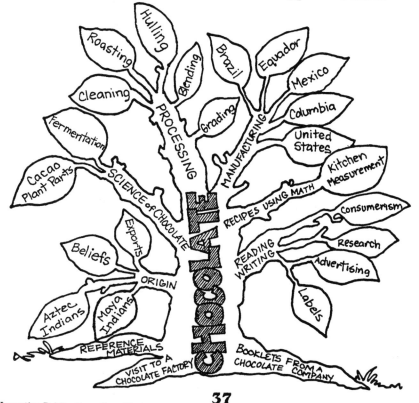

Graphic Organizers and Planning Outlines

Page 41

Interdisciplinary Wheel

For Teachers

The Interdisciplinary Wheel is another planning tool for teachers. Write the name of the interdisciplinary theme or topic to be studied in the small circle in the center of the wheel. Write the name of a subject area at the top of each wedge. Related topics, concepts, skills, and/or activities can be recorded within the appropriate wedges so that one can tell at a glance what the primary content, tasks, and resources will be for this interdisciplinary unit of instruction. A sample Interdisciplinary Wheel is shown below.

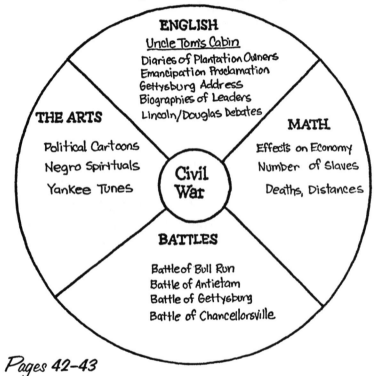

Pages 42–43

Planning Outline
for an Extended Interdisciplinary Unit

For Teachers

This planning outline will get you started on creating an extended interdisciplinary unit. Fill in the lines and build your unit!

Page 44

Interdisciplinary Team Evaluation Report

For Teachers

This form provides a way for each teacher on an interdisciplinary team to contribute to the evaluation of a student's performance.

Graphic Organizers and Planning Outlines

Building an
Interdisciplinary Planning Matrix

Directions on page 37

Content Area	SEPT	OCT	NOV	DEC	JAN	FEB	MAR	APR	MAY
SCIENCE									
MATH									
SOCIAL STUDIES									
LANGUAGE ARTS									
EXPLORATORY									
P. E.									

Directions on page 37

Interdisciplinary Tree

Directions on page 38

Interdisciplinary Wheel

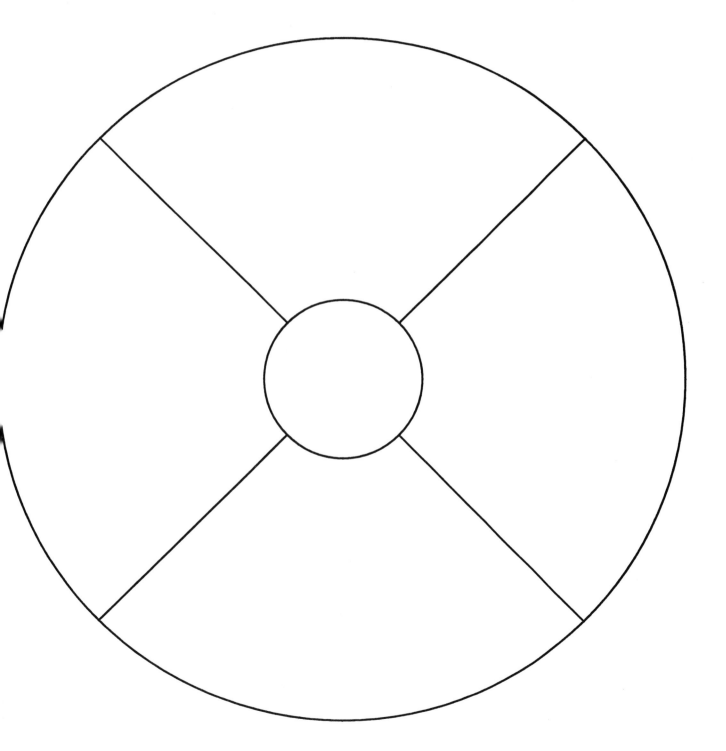

Directions on page 38

Planning Outline for an Extended Interdisciplinary Unit

Title:_____

_____

Theme:_____

_____

Objectives: _____

_____

_____

_____

Background Information for Students: _____

_____

_____

_____

_____

Glossary: _____

_____

_____

_____

Activities in Each Discipline (include title, objective,
materials needed, procedure, and evaluation for each): _____

_____

_____

_____

(continued on next page)

Directions on page 38

Interdisciplinary Unit Outline, Page 2

_____

_____

_____

_____

_____

Homework and/or Enrichment Ideas:_____

_____

_____

_____

_____

_____

Directions for Post-Test or Project Presentation: _____

_____

_____

_____

_____

Bibliography: _____

_____

_____

_____

_____

_____

Directions on page 38

Interdisciplinary Team Evaluation Report

NAME _____

TIME _____ DAY _____ DATE _____

This form is designed to inform you of your child's performance in his or her academic work and/or his or her citizenship for _____ marking period. Circled areas apply at this time. The evaluation scale is as follows:

1 – Excellent   2 – Satisfactory   3 – Needs Improvement   4 – Unsatisfactory

	MATH	ENGLISH	SOCIAL STUDIES	SCIENCE
1. Preparation for class	1 2 3 4	1 2 3 4	1 2 3 4	1 2 3 4
2. Completion of required work	1 2 3 4	1 2 3 4	1 2 3 4	1 2 3 4
3. Attentiveness in class	1 2 3 4	1 2 3 4	1 2 3 4	1 2 3 4
4. Study habits	1 2 3 4	1 2 3 4	1 2 3 4	1 2 3 4
5. Class participation	1 2 3 4	1 2 3 4	1 2 3 4	1 2 3 4
6. Test results	1 2 3 4	1 2 3 4	1 2 3 4	1 2 3 4
7. Punctuality	1 2 3 4	1 2 3 4	1 2 3 4	1 2 3 4
8. Self-discipline	1 2 3 4	1 2 3 4	1 2 3 4	1 2 3 4
9. Cooperation	1 2 3 4	1 2 3 4	1 2 3 4	1 2 3 4
10. Courtesy	1 2 3 4	1 2 3 4	1 2 3 4	1 2 3 4
11. Respect for rights of others	1 2 3 4	1 2 3 4	1 2 3 4	1 2 3 4
12. Respect for school property	1 2 3 4	1 2 3 4	1 2 3 4	1 2 3 4
13. Attitude	1 2 3 4	1 2 3 4	1 2 3 4	1 2 3 4
14. Organization	1 2 3 4	1 2 3 4	1 2 3 4	1 2 3 4
15. Classroom behavior	1 2 3 4	1 2 3 4	1 2 3 4	1 2 3 4
16. Grade to date				

COMMENTS

_____
Team Teacher, Math

_____
Team Teacher, English

_____
Team Teacher, Social Studies

_____
Team Teacher, Science

If necessary, your child's advisory teacher, elective area teacher, and physical education teacher have made comments.

_____
Parent signature

Planning Forms and Outlines

Page 47

My Personal Project Plan

For Students

Use this form to map out a "game plan" for completing a special project in the classroom. Be specific when describing the details of your plan.

Page 48

Plan for Learning Vocabulary

For Students

Use this form for learning terms and vocabulary words associated with a unit of study in any subject area. Choose four words to learn. Write down each word along with its definition. Next, locate a sentence from your textbook in which the word is used and copy the sentence. For future reference, write down the page number on which the sentence was found.

Page 49

Scope and Sequence Ladder

For Students

The Scope and Sequence Ladder can be used for creating a timeline, organizing a sequence of events, or outlining a series of steps to perform a task. On the first rung of the ladder, write the first date, event, or step of your task. On the second rung of the ladder, write the second date, event, or step of your task. Continue in this way with the third, fourth, and fifth rungs. You may use additional ladders if you have a need for more rungs in your planning.

Page 50

A Three-Level Outline

For Students

The Three-Level Outline can be used to plan a report, speech, story, or research project. Record information from your reading and thinking on a topic of your choice using the appropriate lines for major ideas and supporting details.

Planning Tree

For Students

Use the Planning Tree as a tool for planning and completing a project that has a major goal and subgoals to accomplish through a variety of sequential tasks. Write your major goal in the large box. Write your subgoals in the medium-sized boxes. Finally, organize the sequence of tasks for the implementation of the goals in the smaller boxes. It is important that each set of tasks be grouped with the appropriate subgoal in the diagram.

Getting to Know You

For Parents and Students

This form should be sent home so that parents and students may complete it before a scheduled conference.

Parent Post-Conference Form

For Parents

This form is designed for parent/child communication.

Student Post-Conference Form

For Students

The student should be encouraged to complete this reflection form at the end of a student/parent/teacher conference session. It allows the student to share his or her perceptions of the conference dialogue and prescribed outcomes.

Directions on page 45

My Personal Project Plan

PERSONAL PROJECT PLAN

WHAT WILL I DO?	WITH WHOM WILL I WORK?	WHEN WILL I START AND WHEN WILL I FINISH?
	WHERE WILL I LOCATE RESOURCES?	
WHAT PROBLEMS MIGHT I ENCOUNTER?		
	HOW WILL I EVALUATE MY RESULTS?	

Directions on page 45

Plan for Learning Vocabulary

TOPIC/UNIT OF STUDY: _____

1. Term: _____

   Definition: _____

   _____

   _____

   Textbook sentence: _____

   _____

   _____

   _____ Found on page _____

2. Term: _____

   Definition: _____

   _____

   _____

   Textbook sentence: _____

   _____

   _____

   _____ Found on page _____

3. Term: _____

   Definition: _____

   _____

   _____

   Textbook sentence: _____

   _____

   _____

   _____ Found on page _____

Directions on page 45

Scope and Sequence Ladder

5

4

3

2

1

Directions on page 45

A Three-Level Outline

I. _____
  A. _____
    1. _____
    2. _____
    3. _____
  B. _____
    1. _____
    2. _____
    3. _____
  C. _____
    1. _____
    2. _____
    3. _____

II. _____
  A. _____
    1. _____
    2. _____
    3. _____
  B. _____
    1. _____
    2. _____
    3. _____
  C. _____
    1. _____
    2. _____
    3. _____

III. _____
  A. _____
    1. _____
    2. _____
    3. _____
  B. _____
    1. _____
    2. _____
    3. _____
  C. _____
    1. _____
    2. _____
    3. _____

Directions on page 46

Planning Tree

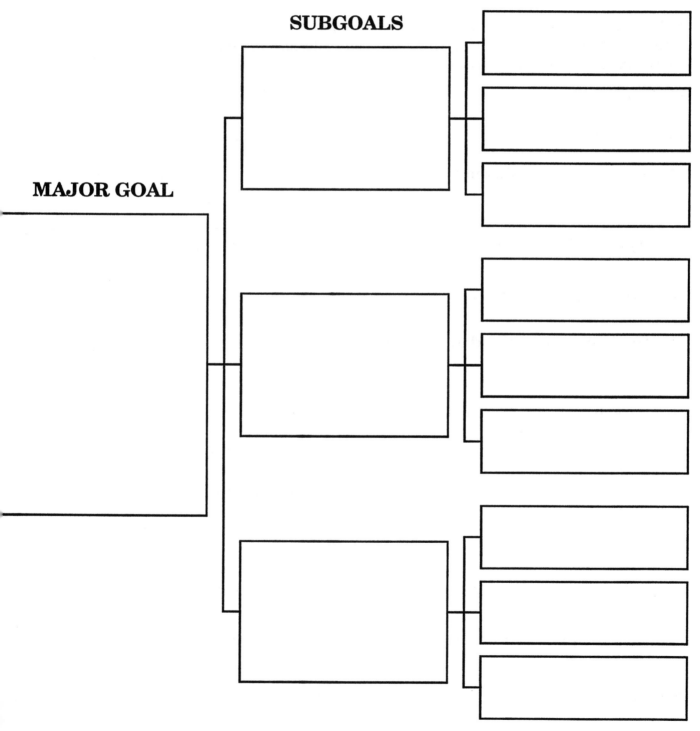

MAJOR GOAL

SUBGOALS

TASKS

Directions on page 46

Getting to Know You

A Collaborative Inventory for Students and Their Parents to Complete

DIRECTIONS: Please take a few minutes to complete this "Getting to Know You" conference form. I will be scheduling a visit with you soon to discuss the information so that we can cooperatively plan for a productive school year.

Student's Name: _____ Date: _____

Parent/Guardian's Name(s): _____

1. My child has the following interests, hobbies, and extracurricular activities outside of school: _____

   _____

2. My child's biggest strengths and successes in school seem to be: _____

   _____

3. One thing my child worries most about in school is: _____

   _____

4. My child works well with teachers who: _____

   _____

   _____

5. If you have to discipline my child in school, my child and I prefer that you (check all that apply):
   __ Use a time-out chair/room   __ Administer grounding at home or
   __ Lecture (in a nice way)   school
   __ Take away school/home privileges   __ Contact the home immediately and
   __ Scold (not in so nice a way)   leave discipline to us

   Other (please specify): _____

   _____

6. The most important thing we all want from this year's schooling experience is: _____

   _____

7. The best times/days for a parent/student/teacher conference are: _____

   _____

Signed: _____   Signed: _____
             Parent/Guardian   Student

Directions on page 46

Parent Post-Conference Form

1. During the conference, I noticed that _____
   _____
   _____

2. During the conference, I felt proud because _____
   _____
   _____

3. I am pleased to see your extra effort in _____
   _____
   _____

4. I know you sometimes had difficulty, but _____
   _____
   _____

5. I am proud of your improvement in _____
   _____
   _____

6. I can help you by _____
   _____
   _____

53

Directions on page 46

Student Post-Conference Form

1. Things went smoothly during the conference because _____

    _____

    _____

2. Things could have gone better if _____

    _____

    _____

3. One thing I wish I would have shared with my parents, but forgot: _____

    _____

    _____

4. One thing I chose not to share, but should have: _____

    _____

    _____

5. As I look back on what I gained from being actively involved in my conference, I notice

    _____

    _____

6. Something I feel my parents gained from hearing things from my point of view: _____

    _____

    _____

7. I felt that my teachers _____

    _____

    _____

Research and Study Aids

Page 59

Cause-and-Effect Chain

For Students

Use the appropriate sections of the chain to record a series of cause-and-effect relationships learned from a topic of study. Be sure that each CAUSE produces a related EFFECT and that all of the CAUSES lead to the ultimate or final EFFECT.

Page 60

Compare and Contrast Chart

For Students

Use the chart to record similarities and differences among states, countries, or continents.

Page 61

Compare and Contrast Diagram

For Students

Use this organizer when you want to relate a new concept you are researching or learning to knowledge you already have on a related concept. Concept 1 and Concept 2 should be recorded in the two rectangles at the top of the page.

Comparison step:	Write how the two concepts are similar in the HOW ALIKE? box.
Contrast step:	Note the differences between the two concepts in the HOW DIFFERENT? columns.

Page 62

Cycle Graph

For Teachers and Students

The Cycle Graph can be used to identify events that tend to be circular or cyclical in nature. Record the title of the topic in the rectangular box. Then list the events or situations that must take place, in sequence, for the cycle to be completed successfully. The first event or situation should be recorded in the top box, with subsequent events or situations recorded in order in the other boxes, moving in a clockwise direction. Additional boxes may be inserted anywhere in the cycle as needed.

Page 63

Fact or Fiction Position Statements

For Students

Record selected statements from readings, discussions, or observations that surface on a topic being studied. Check the appropriate BEFORE box that indicates whether you think the statement is fact or fiction. After doing further clarification of and research on the statement, check the appropriate AFTER box to show whether the statement is indeed fact or fiction.

Page 64

Fishbone Model

For Students

This organizer is good to use when investigating the causes of a research problem that involves a cause-and-effect situation. The effect is written in the rectangle at the HEAD of the fish and various categories are written in the rectangles at the ends of the major BONES of the fish. Possible causes of the effect are recorded on the SMALLER BONES under the most appropriate category names.

Page 65

5 Ws and How Model

For Students

This is a good research aid for students when the topic under study is narrow and specific. Write the topic on the line provided and record the 5 Ws and How of the topic in the appropriate boxes. Finally, write a comprehensive Summary Statement using the information on the chart.

Page 66

Flowchart

For Teachers and Students

This is an instructional page. Flowcharts are used to organize sequences of events, actions, or decisions. A standard set of symbols is used when designing flowcharts so that they can be understood by all. The arrangement of the symbols will vary according to the type of sequence depicted. This page explains the symbols and how each one is used. Use a blank piece of paper to create your flowchart.

Issue Identification and Classification Diagram

For Students and Teachers

This is another instructional page. The procedure described is especially helpful when a small group of students is analyzing a large or complex issue in social studies, current events, or science classes (such as prejudice, crime, or pollution). It is a good way to organize and understand thoughts and ideas related to issues that may be difficult to grasp.

KWL Chart

For Students

When studying any topic, record facts that are known to you in the first column, things you want to know in the second column, and new facts that you learn in the third column.

Opposing Forces Chart

For Students

This chart is best used in small groups. Use it when you are trying to identify potential causes of and solutions for a problem or important challenge/opportunity. At the top of the chart, write the situation to be resolved or challenge/opportunity goal to be reached. In the arrows under the DRIVING FORCES heading, record as many forces as you can that you think would move you toward your goal or problem solution. (Driving forces are defined as positive actions, skills, people, tools, and procedures available to you at this time.) In the arrows under the OPPOSING FORCES heading, record as many forces as you can that you think are keeping you from reaching your goal or solving your problem. (Opposing forces can be any restraining actions, skills, people, tools, and procedures that are interfering with your attempts to resolve your situation.) Once the forces have been identified, it is up to you to prioritize the driving and opposing forces and to begin eliminating the problem areas and capitalizing on the positive areas.

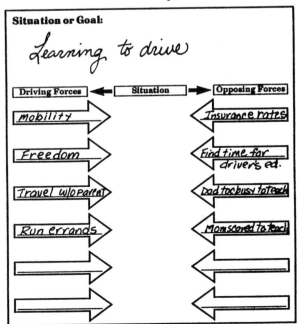

57

Page 70

Person Pyramid

For Students

Use the pyramid figure to record important information about a person. This can be a tool for organizing data collected on an individual the student is researching for a report such as a biography book report or a social studies famous leader report.

Pages 71-72

SQ3R Chart

For Students

This chart is helpful when reading a chapter from a textbook. Use one chart for each major section of the chapter.

Page 73

Steps to Take in the Analysis of a Piece of Literature

For Students

Use the steps on the diagram to analyze the major parts of a short story, novel, or poem. Write down details, descriptions, events, clue words, traits, attributes, or ideas that summarize the elements of the piece of literature.

Pages 74-75

Worksheet for Implementation of Cause-and-Effect Model

For Students

This worksheet may be used when investigating causes, effects, and possible solutions for a given problem. It is particularly effective when used by cooperative learning groups.

Page 76

Venn Diagram

For Students

A Venn diagram is useful when researching a topic that requires comparison and contrast. As you conduct the research, look for interrelationships among subtopics. Record areas of commonality in the intersecting segments of the circles and record differences in the appropriate nonintersecting segments of the circles.

Directions on page 55

Cause-and-Effect Chain

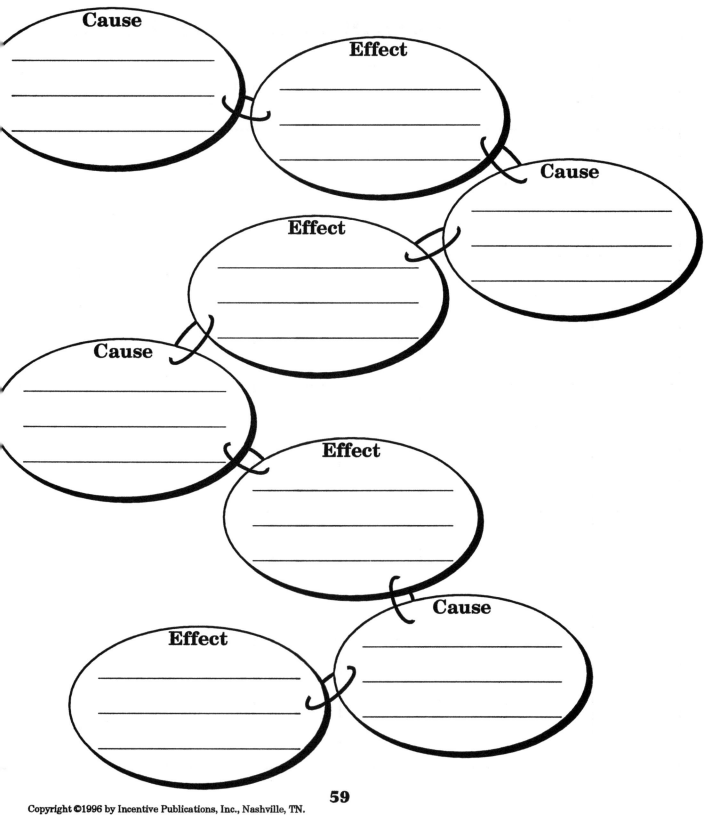

Directions on page 55

Compare and Contrast Chart

SIMILARITIES AND DIFFERENCES IN PLACES

Name	Location	Population	Area	Major Cities	Major Industries	Major Features	Major Facts

Directions on page 55

Compare and Contrast Diagram

Concept 1 _____

Concept 2 _____

HOW ALIKE?

_____

_____

_____

_____

_____

HOW DIFFERENT?
With Regard To

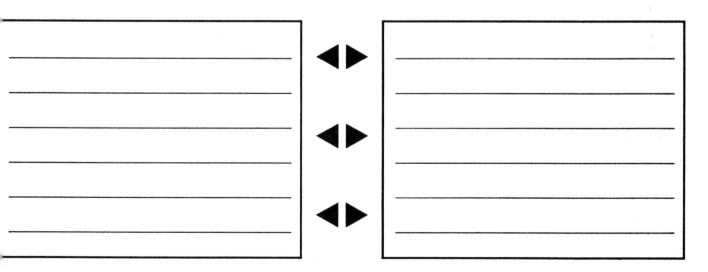

Directions on page 55

Cycle Graph

TITLE

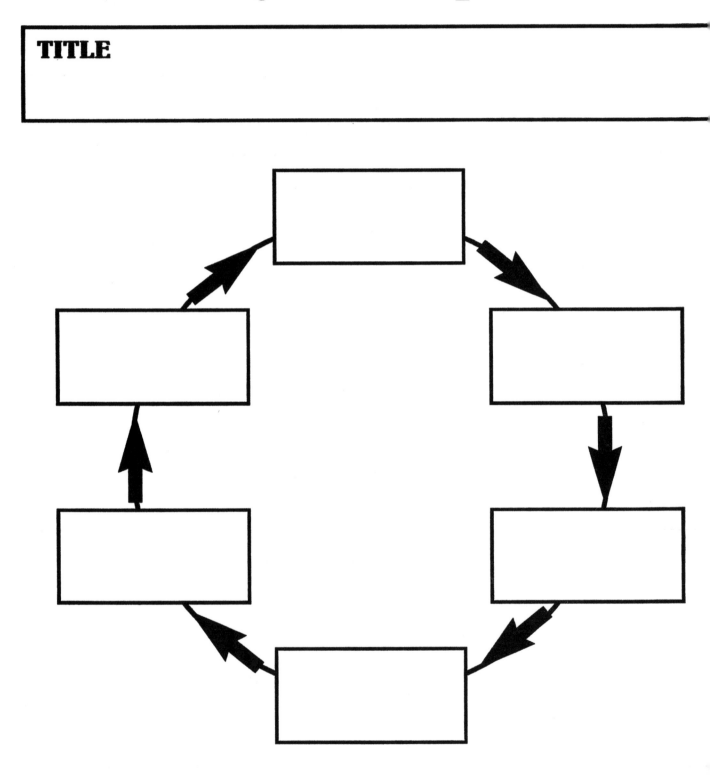

Directions on page 56

Fact or Fiction Position Statements

Topic: _____

Statement	Before		After	
	Fact	Fiction	Fact	Fiction
1.				
2.				
3.				
4.				
5.				
6.				
7.				
8.				

Fishbone Model

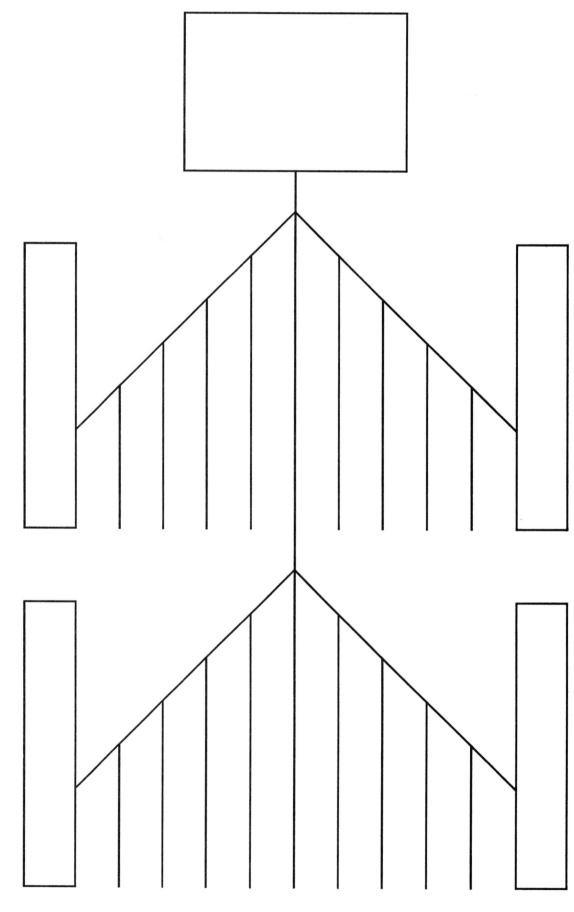

Directions on page 56

Directions on page 56

5 Ws and How Model

TOPIC: _____

Who:	**What:**	**When:**	**Where:**	**Why:**	**How:**	**Summary Statement:**

Directions on page 56

Flowchart

Instructions: The question to be answered or the problem to be solved is written in the diamond with yes/no responses recorded in circles, action steps in rectangles, explanations in broken-line rectangles, and answers in trapezoids.

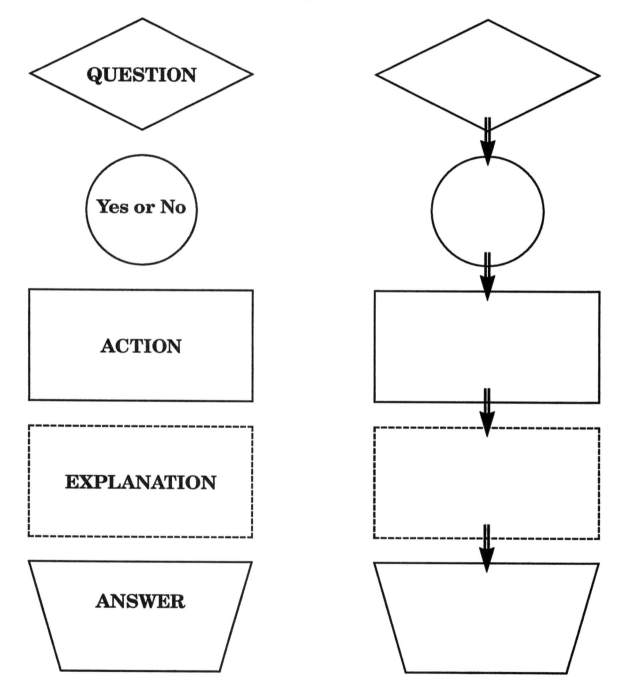

Directions on page 57

Issue Identification and Classification Diagram

1. Write the issue under study at the top of a large sheet of chart paper.
2. Give each member of the group a small package of file cards or sticky notes. Each person is to spend approximately three minutes writing down a series of thoughts or ideas related to the issue. These idea statements should be listed in no more than three words and only one idea per card or sticky note. All cards or notes should be placed randomly on the chart paper as they are completed. There is to be no talking during this part of the activity.
3. Participants should collectively classify and arrange the cards or sticky notes into columns of related groups and create a title or heading for each column/group. The headings should be short, and similar groups should be placed next to each other.
4. Once the group members have agreed on the classification scheme, research and reports can be assigned according to topic or category.

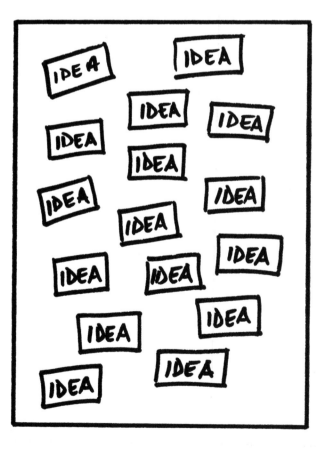

Directions on page 57

KWL Chart

TOPIC: _____

Know	Want to Know	Learned

Directions on page 57

Opposing Forces Chart

Situation or Goal:

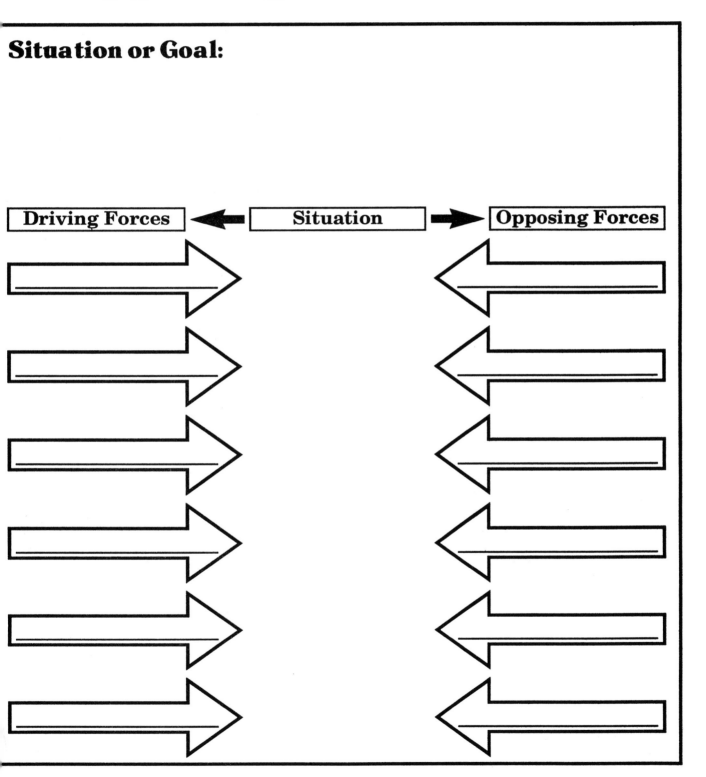

| Driving Forces | ← Situation → | Opposing Forces |

Directions on page 58

Person Pyramid

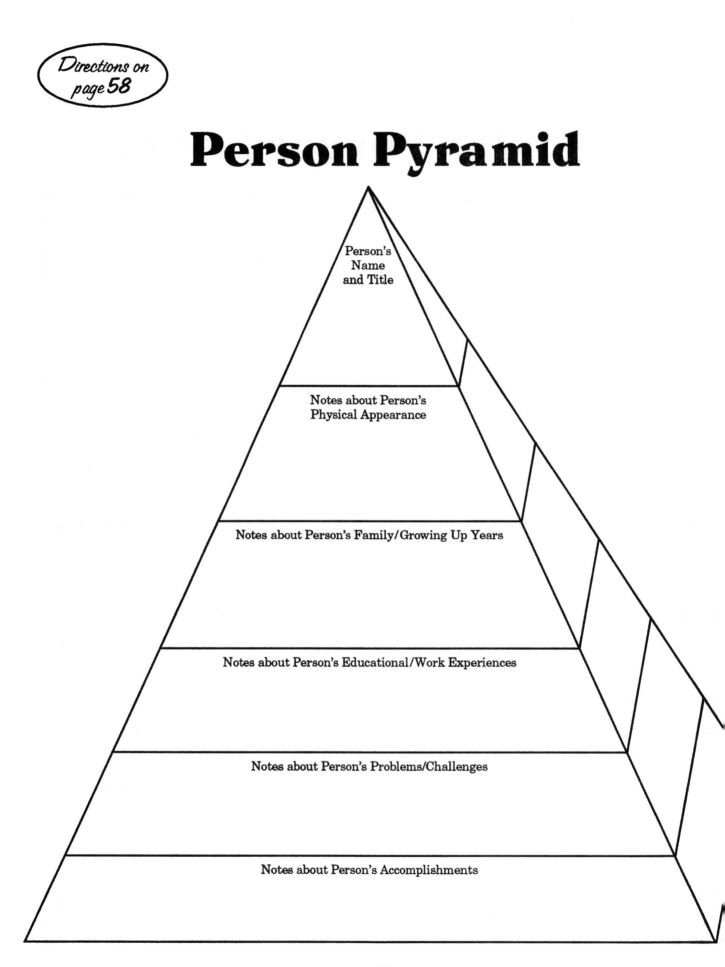

Person's Name and Title

Notes about Person's Physical Appearance

Notes about Person's Family/Growing Up Years

Notes about Person's Educational/Work Experiences

Notes about Person's Problems/Challenges

Notes about Person's Accomplishments

Directions on page 58

SQ3R Chart

Directions

This chart is helpful when reading a chapter from a textbook. Use one chart for each major section of the chapter. Remember that SQ3R means:

Survey: Read titles/subtitles. Notice words/phrases in special type. Skim illustrations/ charts/graphs. Review end-of-chapter summaries and questions.

Question: Turn main/subtopics in special print into 5W questions—Who, What, When, Where, and Why.

Read: Read information to answer questions, highlighting main ideas and taking notes.

Recite: Pause at the end of each chapter section to orally answer questions, using your own words.

Review: Construct a study guide sheet that includes summaries and main ideas from your reading.

Survey: Record most important titles and subtitles from major chapter section.

_____

_____

_____

_____

_____

_____

Question: Write Who, What, When, Where, and Why questions for main/subtopics.

_____

_____

_____

_____

_____

_____

71

Directions on page 58

Read: Write short answers to five questions from above.

_____

_____

_____

_____

_____

_____

_____

_____

Recite: Record additional facts and cue phrases as needed for each question.

_____

_____

_____

_____

_____

_____

_____

_____

Review: Compose a short summary paragraph for each question. Staple your pages together as a study guide.

_____

_____

_____

_____

_____

_____

_____

_____

_____

Directions on page 58

Steps to Take in the Analysis of a Piece of Literature

Climax

Conflict
_____
_____
_____
_____

Falling Action
_____
_____
_____
_____

Antagonist
_____
_____
_____
_____
_____

Point of View
_____
_____
_____
_____
_____

Protagonist
_____
_____
_____
_____
_____
_____

Theme
_____
_____
_____
_____
_____
_____

Setting
_____
_____
_____
_____
_____

Ending
_____
_____
_____
_____
_____

Directions on page 58

Worksheet for Implementation of Cause-and-Effect Model

Problem Topic: _____

Stating the Problem:

Write down two complete sentences briefly describing the problem to be solved.

_____

_____

_____

_____

_____

Determining the Satisfaction Level:

Make a list of undesirable effects of the problem, and then make another list of desirable outcomes that would happen if the problem were solved.

_____

_____

_____

_____

_____

Locating the Multiple Causes:

Write down all of the possible causes of the problem and place an asterisk (*) next to those items that represent the most likely causes of the problem.

_____

_____

_____

_____

_____

74

Directions on page 58

Worksheet for Implementation of Cause-and-Effect Model, Page 2

Considering Optional Solutions:

Record all possible solutions or courses of action that one might take to solve the problem.

_____

_____

_____

_____

_____

Establishing Solution Criteria:

Develop a set of criteria and a rating scale by which to evaluate the criteria and select the best solution for the problem.

_____

_____

_____

_____

_____

Finding a Solution:

Apply the criteria and rating scale to each of the possible solutions and decide which one best addresses your problem statement.

_____

_____

_____

_____

_____

Venn Diagram

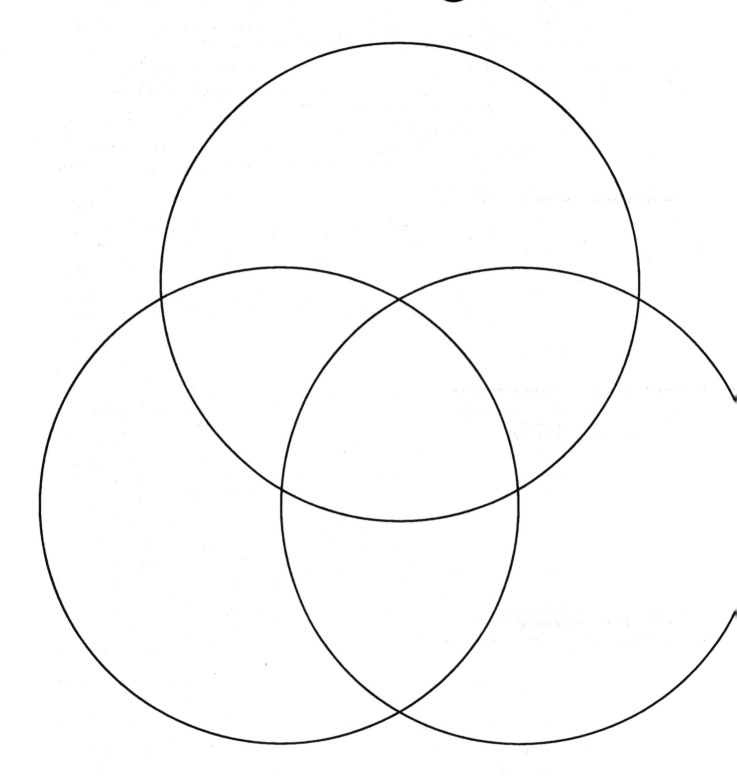

The Web

Page 79

Web

For Teachers and Students

This tool is helpful for brainstorming and generating multiple ideas on a given topic or organizing information in a current topic of study. The major topic is written in the large circle in the center of the diagram. Important ideas related to the major topic are written in the rectangles adjacent to the circle, and additional subtopics are recorded in the rectangles at the end of each line. The final effect will be one of ideas emanating from the circle much like spokes on a wheel.

Page 80

Attribute Diagram

For Students

Use the Attribute Diagram when you need to identify distinguishing characteristics of an object, plant, animal, or mineral. In the circle, write the name of the item being analyzed. On the six spokes radiating from the circle, write the major characteristics or descriptors of the item. On the lines extending from the spokes, record a set of details related to each major characteristic or descriptor.

Page 81

The 5 Ws and How Web Process

For Students

Use this web to record the 5 Ws and How of a magazine article, a newspaper article, or an excerpt from a classroom textbook. Write the article or chapter title in the center hexagon and answer the questions about the situation in the appropriate web sections. Then create a paragraph summarizing the information from this web.

Page 82

Constructing a Mind Map

For Teachers and Students

This type of freehand web can be easily created following the directions and illustration on page 82.

Page 83

Organizing Tree

For Students

Use the tree outline to organize information and structure your ideas on a topic in any content area. Write the major topic in the oval at the top of the tree, subheadings in other ovals, and information on diagonals extending from the subheadings.

Page 84

Prediction Tree

For Students

The Prediction Tree is a web with a purpose. Write the major topic or problem under discussion as a question in the square box at the bottom of the tree. Brainstorm possible predictions or probable outcomes in response to the question and record these in the prediction boxes. On the proof lines, record facts that either support or negate the predictions.

Directions on page 77

Web

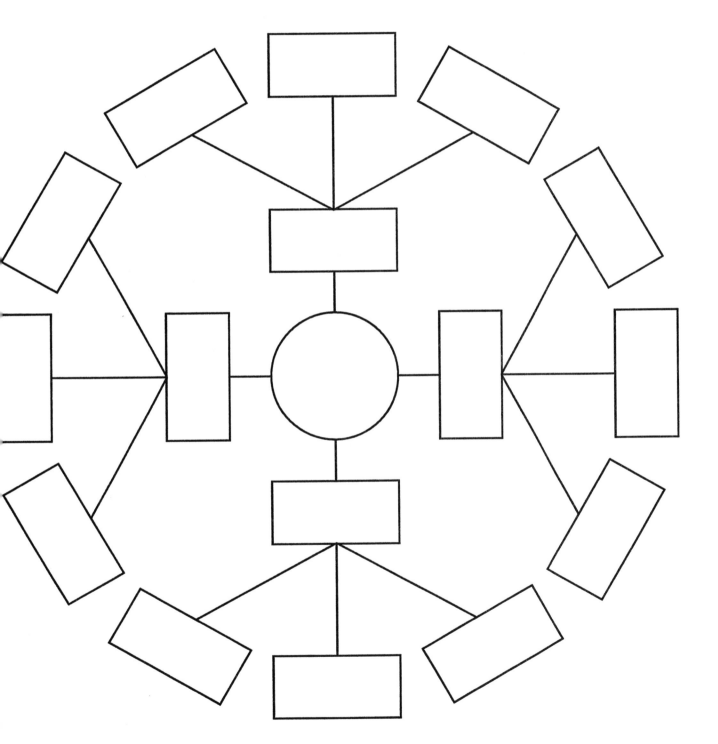

Directions on page 77

Attribute Diagram

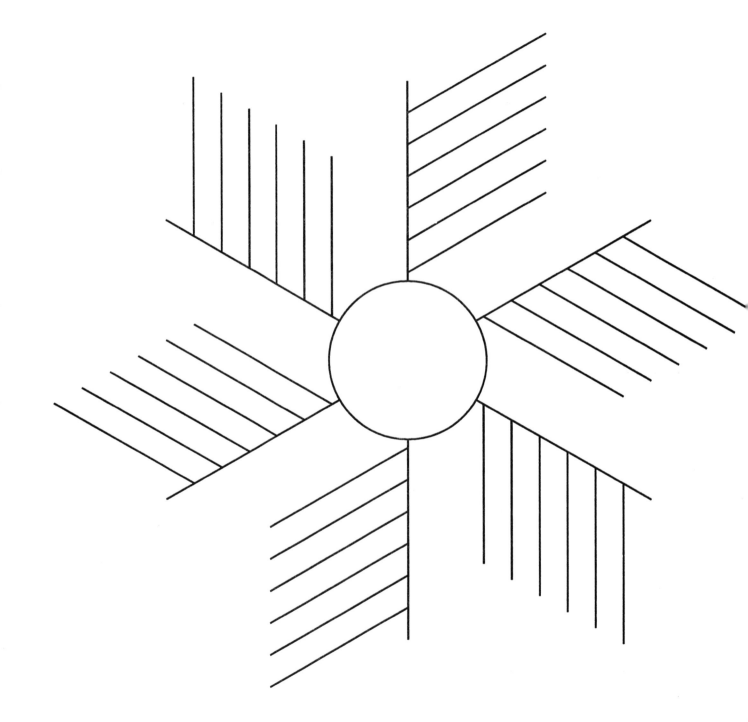

Directions on page 77

The Five Ws and How Web Process

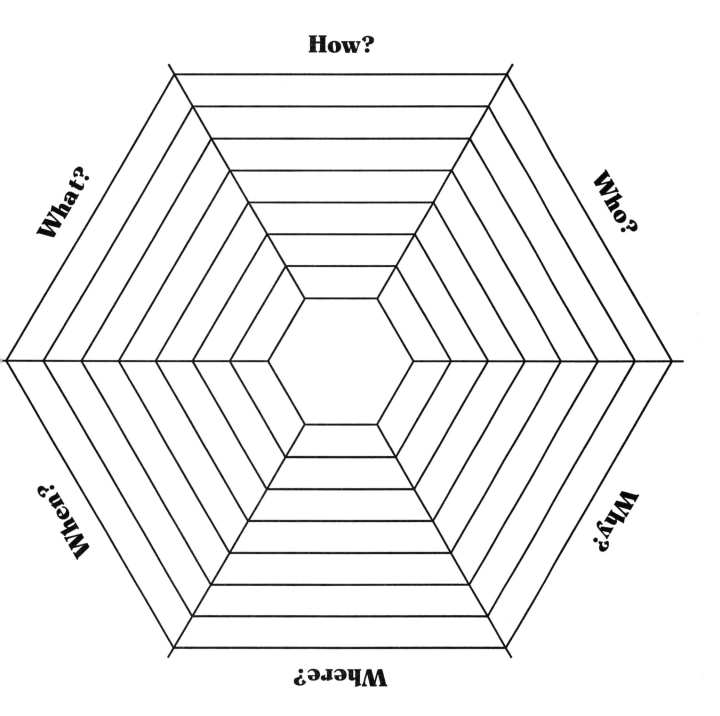

How?

What?

Who?

When?

Why?

Where?

Directions on page 78

Constructing a Mind Map

DIRECTIONS

A mind map is a graphic illustration of major ideas around a central topic or theme.
Mind maps are useful tools in helping us draw a global picture of a concept for ourselves.
The steps for constructing a mind map are:

1. In the middle of the page, write out the major topic, idea, or concept to be studied.
   Put a colored circle around the topic.

2. Identify subtopics related to the main idea in the circle. Write down a key word or
   brief phrase describing each subtopic. Circle each subtopic with a colored pencil an
   draw a spoke out from the main idea. Put related ideas in circles of the same color.
   Keep the number of key words/phrases to a minimum.

3. Remember that mind maps use colorful pictures/circles to provide you with visual
   clues for recalling the essence of a concept, idea, or thought.

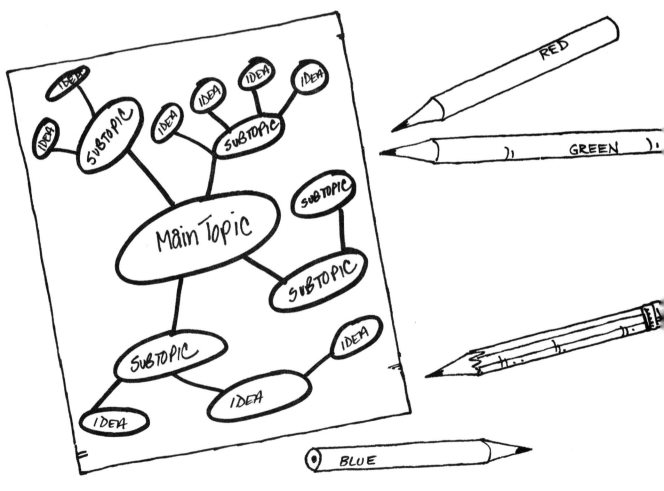

Directions on page 78

Organizing Tree

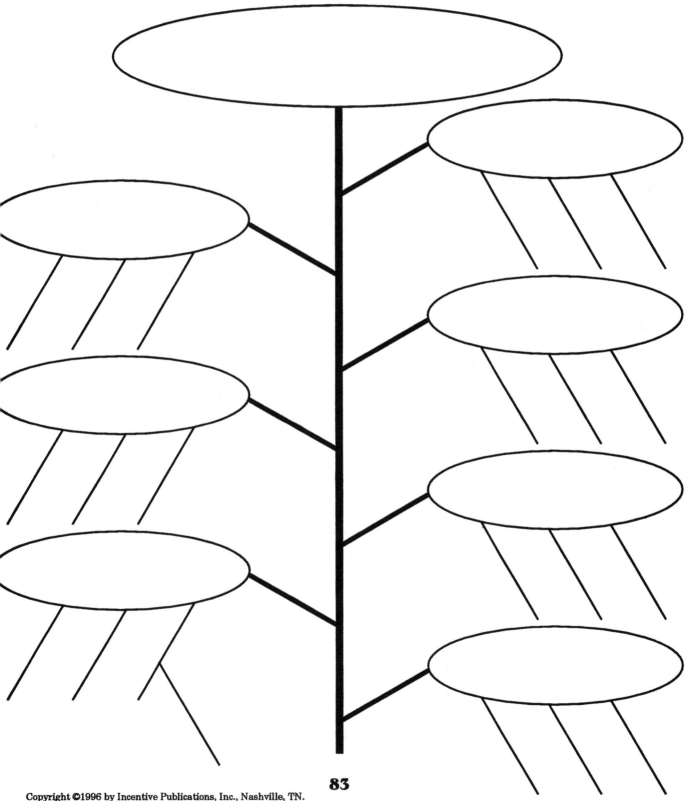

Directions on page 78

Prediction Tree

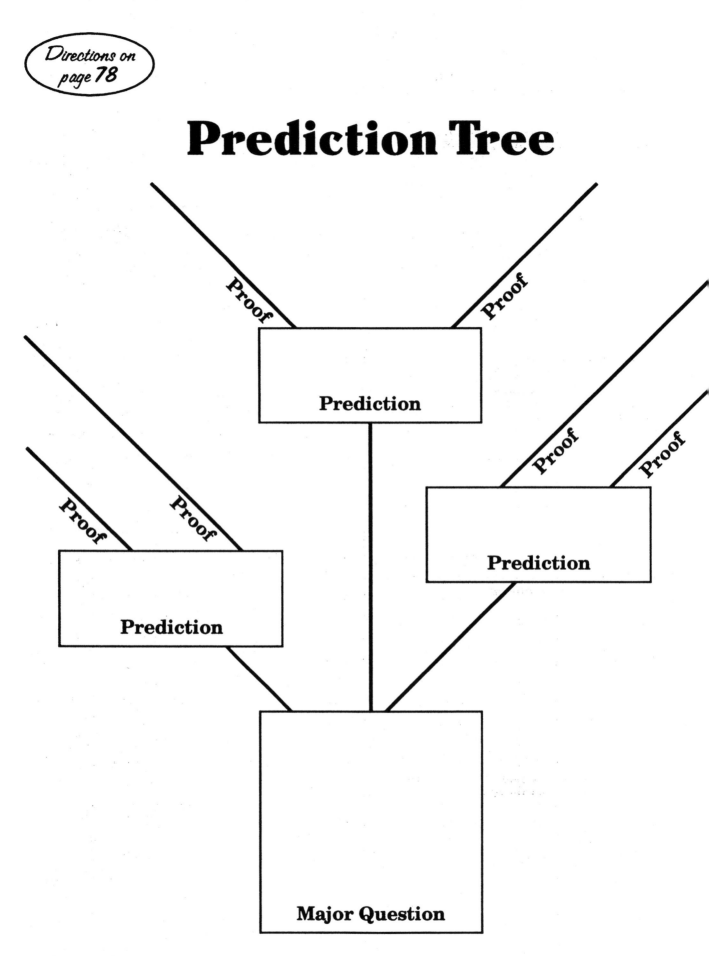

Proof

Proof

Prediction

Proof

Proof

Proof

Proof

Prediction

Prediction

Major Question

Writing Planners
and Organizers

Page 87

Book Report Outline for Use with
Any Content Topic

For Students

This book report form uses Bloom's Taxonomy as its organizing structure.

Page 88

Book Report Pyramid

For Students

Here's another way to write a book report. Start at the bottom of the pyramid and work your way up!

Pages 89–90

My Plan for Writing a Novel

For Students

Use this planning form to outline the setting, plot, and characterization of each chapter in your novel.

Page 91

Planning Worksheet for Writing an Essay

For Students

This worksheet will help you get started when your assignment is to write an essay.

Page 92

Reporter's Triangle

For Students

The Reporter's Triangle at the top of the page illustrates the relative importance of the various components of an article written by a journalist. Keeping this information in mind, fill in the lines on the rest of the page in preparation for the writing of your article. This information and procedure can also be used when the assignment is to create a television advertisement.

Page 93

The Umbrella

For Students

Sometimes we refer to the big idea or main concept of a topic as the umbrella theme. The Umbrella can help you organize your thoughts when you must write a report or essay. Inside the umbrella outline, write the big idea or main concept in two or three sentences. On the lines adjacent to the handle of the umbrella, write as many details or related thoughts as you can. You might want to prioritize these in some way such as putting the major details on one side of the handle and the minor details on the other side of the handle. Or you may decide to order the ideas from most important to least important using a number scale.

Directions on page 85

Book Report Outline For Use with Any Content Topic

DIRECTIONS:
Select a nonfiction book on the topic of your choice and use it to complete the activities below.

KNOWLEDGE
1. Record the answers to each of the following questions.
What is the title of the book?
Who wrote the book?
When was the book published?
Where did you locate the book?

COMPREHENSION
2. Summarize the main ideas or facts found in the book.

APPLICATION
3. Select several key words or terms from the book and classify them in some way.

ANALYSIS
4. Compare your book with another book on the same topic. How are the books alike and how are they different?

SYNTHESIS
5. Suppose that you were to write a new book on this topic. Create an original book jacket for your masterpiece.

EVALUATION
6. Would you recommend the book to anyone else? Give three to five reasons for your choice.

Directions on page 85

Book Report Pyramid

Name _____

Start at the bottom of the pyramid and work your way up to the top.

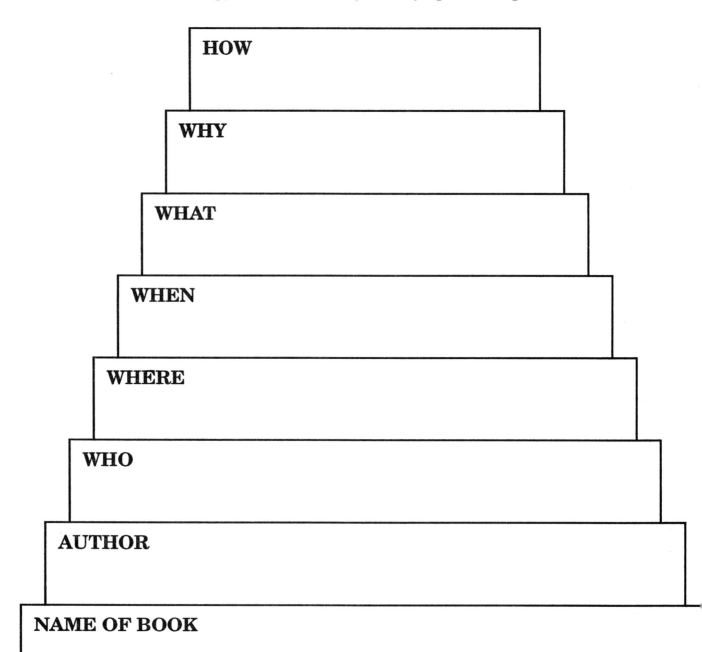

HOW

WHY

WHAT

WHEN

WHERE

WHO

AUTHOR

NAME OF BOOK

Directions on page 85

My Plan for Writing a Novel

1. What is my working title for this chapter?

    _____

    _____

    _____

2. How did I end the preceding chapter?

    _____

    _____

    _____

    _____

3. How will I begin this new chapter? (If possible, compose the opening sentence or paragraph.)

    _____

    _____

    _____

    _____

4. What is the setting for this chapter?

    _____

    _____

    _____

    _____

Directions on page 85

5. What is the major action to be described in this chapter and how will the main character(s) be involved?

_____

_____

_____

_____

_____

6. What are the sequences of events for this major action?

_____

_____

_____

_____

_____

7. How will I end this chapter? (If possible, compose the closing sentence or **paragraph**.)

_____

_____

_____

_____

8. How will the next chapter begin?

_____

_____

_____

_____

Directions on page 85

Planning Worksheet for Writing an Essay

1. What are several topics I may consider for my essay? (I will put a star by the one I select.)

    _____

    _____

    _____

2. What are some of my opinions concerning this topic?

    _____

    _____

    _____

3. Will I need to do any research in order to find supporting facts for my opinions? How will I go about conducting my research?

    _____

    _____

    _____

4. What is the most important sentence in my essay? (This may be used as the **very first** sentence; wherever it is placed, it should state the major premise of the essay clearly and well.)

    _____

    _____

    _____

Graphic Organizers and Planning Outlines

Directions on page 86

Reporter's Triangle

Catchy Opening Phrase

Basic Information:
Who, What, When, Where, Why?

Supporting
Details

Less
Important
Facts

Catchy Opening Phrase: _____

_____

_____

Basic Information: Who, What, When, Where, Why? _____

_____

_____

Supporting Details: _____

_____

_____

Less Important Facts: _____

_____

_____

Directions on
page 86

The Umbrella

Index